WHAT GOES
INSIDE?

Albatros

WOOF

Hi there! My name is Bruno.
Has it ever occurred to you
that we're surrounded by things
we can't actually see inside?
I think about it all the time.

What goes inside all these containers?

I've decided to find out.
Would you care to join me?
Let's explore together!

WHAT GOES INSIDE
A FRIDGE?

leek

asparagus

broccoli

avocado

honeydew melon

bananas

pineapple

papaya

apples

strawberries

cabbage

watermelon

artichokes

beetroots

eggplant

cucumbers

oranges

carrots

onions

grapes

pumpkins

tangerines

lemons

bell peppers

frozen vegetables

jams

tomatoes

chili peppers

sardines

canned veggies

mustard

ketchup

soup

salami

steak

salmon

oil

pickles

sausages

ham

fish

juice

milk

water

hot dogs

eggs

butter

yogurt

cheeses

ice cream bars

cake

WHAT GOES INSIDE
A WASHING MACHINE?

parkas

forgotten money

jackets

T-shirts

sweatshirts

scarves

socks

teddy bear

dresses

tank tops

tights

pajamas

washed passports

briefs

boxer shorts

sweaters

onesies

forgotten tissues

panties

shorts

sweat pants

pants

overalls

skirts

WHAT GOES INSIDE
A BATHROOM CABINET?

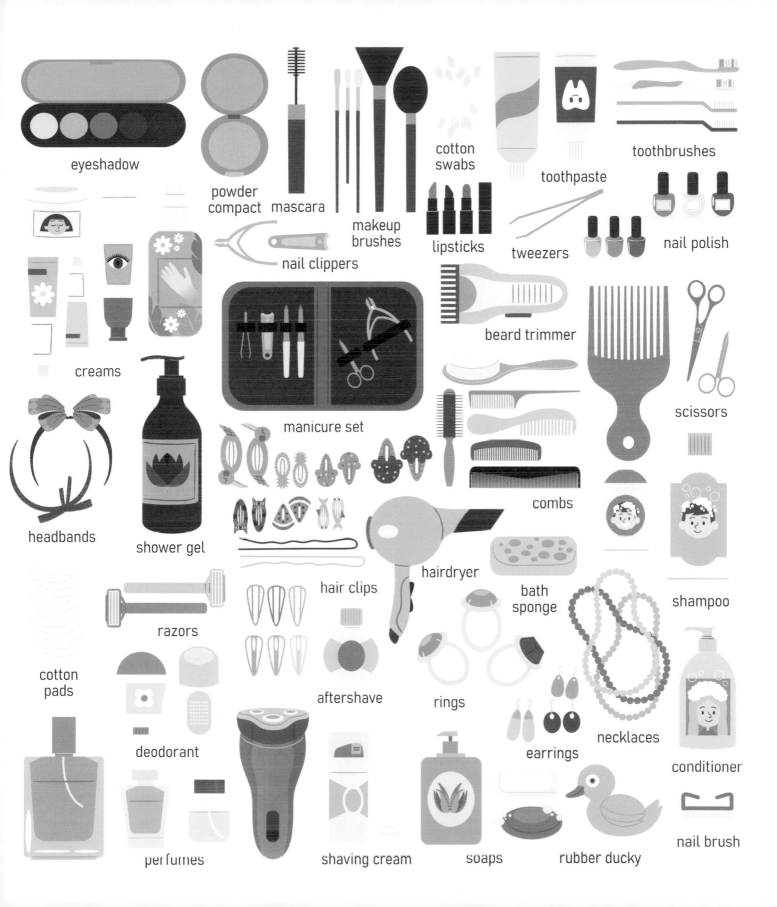

eyeshadow

powder compact

mascara

makeup brushes

cotton swabs

toothpaste

toothbrushes

lipsticks

tweezers

nail polish

nail clippers

creams

manicure set

beard trimmer

scissors

headbands

shower gel

combs

hair clips

hairdryer

bath sponge

shampoo

razors

aftershave

rings

necklaces

conditioner

cotton pads

deodorant

earrings

nail brush

perfumes

shaving cream

soaps

rubber ducky

WHAT GOES INSIDE
A TOOLBOX?

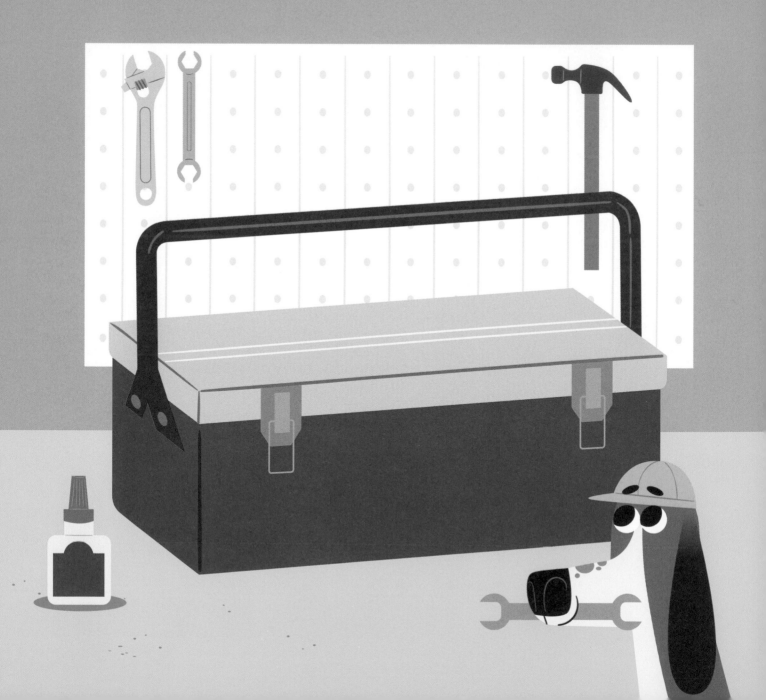

saws

paint rollers

folding meters

pliers

nails, screws, and bolts

plaster

box cutters

eraser

pencils

nuts

wrenches

axes

helmet

adhesive tape

water level

monkey wrenches

screwdrivers

trowels

hammers

flashlight

sandpaper

glue

tape measure

protective glasses

extension cable

gloves

drills

brushes

WHAT GOES INSIDE
A CLASSROOM?

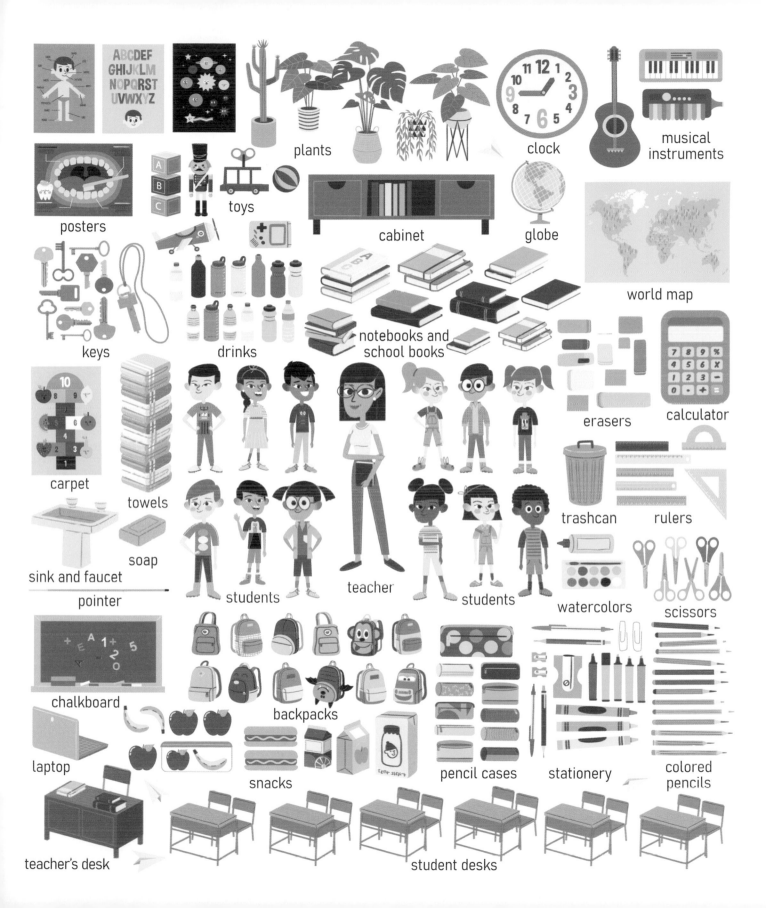

posters

plants

clock

musical instruments

toys

cabinet

globe

world map

keys

drinks

notebooks and school books

erasers

calculator

carpet

towels

soap

sink and faucet

pointer

students

teacher

students

trashcan

rulers

watercolors

scissors

chalkboard

backpacks

pencil cases

stationery

colored pencils

laptop

snacks

teacher's desk

student desks

WHAT GOES INSIDE
A SCHOOL GYM?

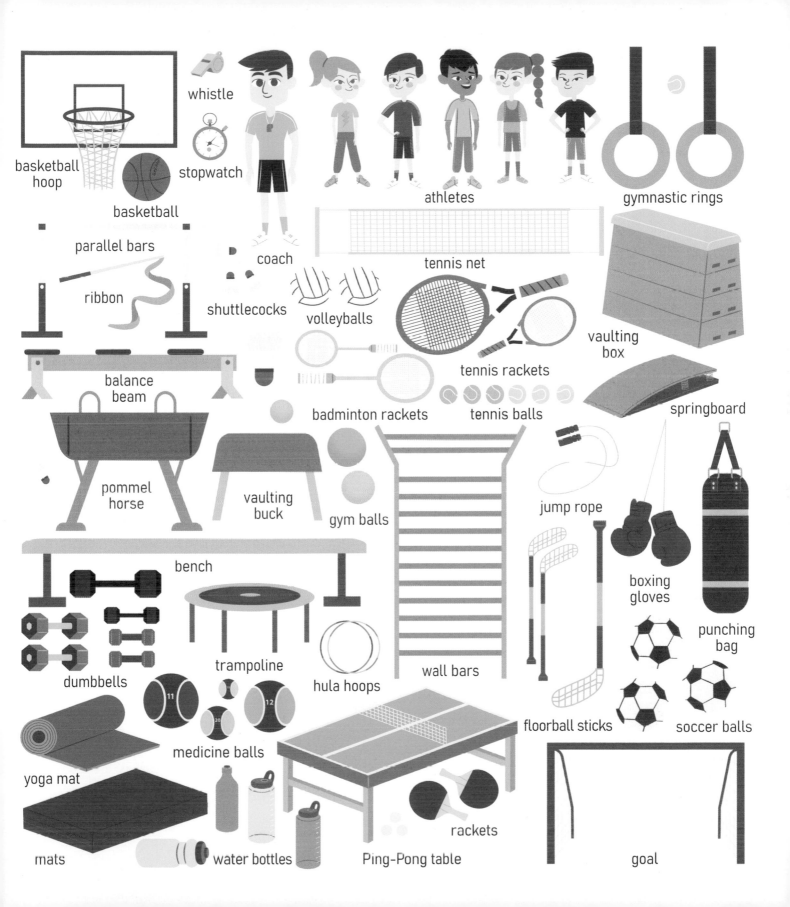

basketball
hoop

basketball

whistle

stopwatch

coach

athletes

gymnastic rings

parallel bars

ribbon

shuttlecocks

volleyballs

tennis net

tennis rackets

vaulting
box

badminton rackets

tennis balls

springboard

balance
beam

pommel
horse

vaulting
buck

gym balls

wall bars

jump rope

boxing
gloves

punching
bag

bench

trampoline

hula hoops

dumbbells

medicine balls

floorball sticks

soccer balls

yoga mat

mats

water bottles

Ping-Pong table

rackets

goal

WHAT GOES INSIDE
A CAMPER?

sunglasses

rug

first-aid kit

fishing rod

backpack

camping furniture

gas stove

shower

road atlas

cards

flashlight

vase

folding stool

mini-fridge

clothes

bed linens

board games

radio

basic foods

bookcase

sofa

canteen

toys

pictures

television

flashlight

toiletries

microwave

bin

lamp

toilet

sink and faucet

towels

sewing kit

dishes

table

slippers

guitar

sun hat

dish towel

WHAT GOES INSIDE
AN IGLOO?

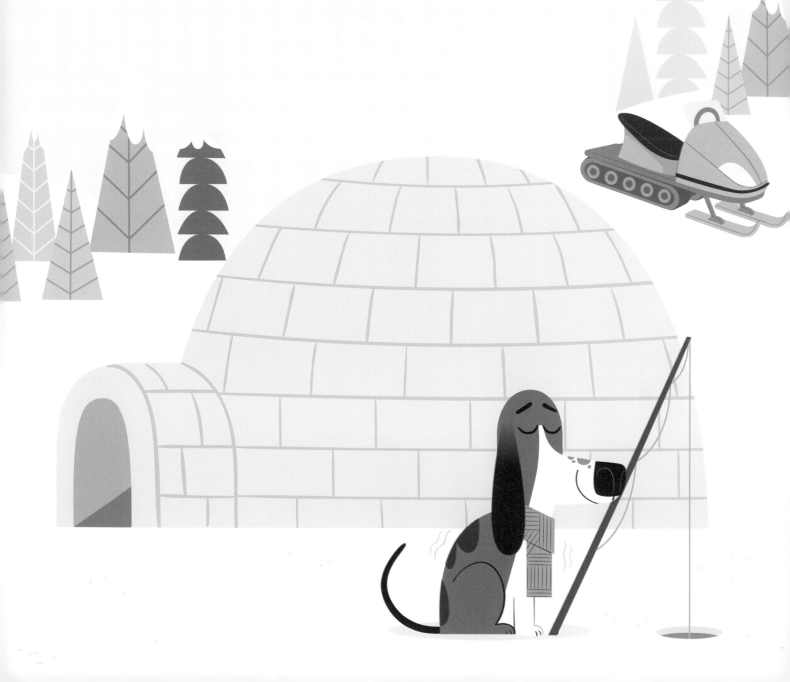

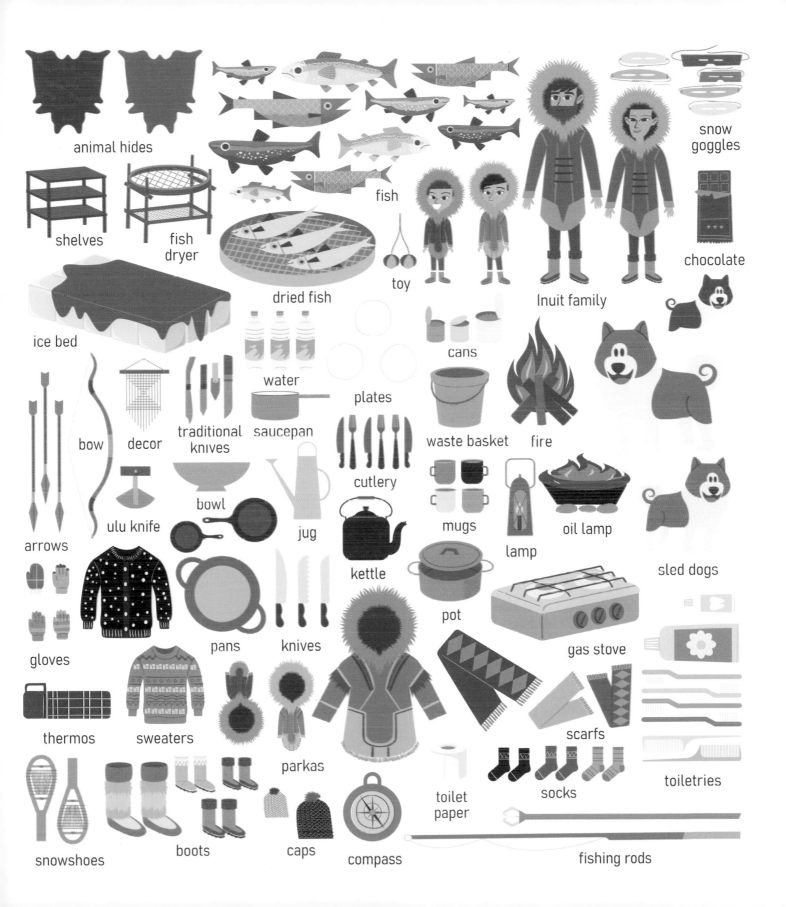

animal hides

fish

snow goggles

shelves

fish dryer

toy

Inuit family

chocolate

dried fish

ice bed

water

plates

cans

bow

decor

traditional knives

saucepan

cutlery

waste basket

fire

bowl

jug

mugs

oil lamp

ulu knife

lamp

arrows

kettle

sled dogs

gloves

pans

knives

pot

gas stove

thermos

sweaters

parkas

scarfs

toiletries

snowshoes

boots

caps

compass

toilet paper

socks

fishing rods

WHAT GOES INSIDE
A PIRATE SHIP?

treasure map

swords and sabers

gems

rat

keys

anchor

rum

compass

stool

bench

watches

rigging

coins

hourglass

blunderbusses

hat

lamp

table

parrot

hammock

quill and ink

ship's wheel

barrels with food

spyglass

pirate kids

cannonballs

monkey

crow's nest

cannon

ship's log

daggers

candlesticks

chest

pirates

prisoner

tableware

WHAT GOES INSIDE
AN HERBARIUM?

ginkgo leaf

oak leaf

maple leaf

lily of the valley

birch leaf

lavender

cowslip

Swiss cheese plant

bellflower

fern

daffodil

mint

sage

basil

red poppy

oregano

ox-eye daisy

scotch tape

chestnut leaf

clover

chamomile

forget-me-not

nettle

snowdrop

dandelion

cornflower

violet

sunflower

thyme

rose

tulip

WHAT GOES INSIDE
A GARDEN SHED?

garden shears

sickles

basket

gloves

rakes

pebbles

fertilizer

bag

lamp

buckets

flower box

seeds

watering can

Earthworms

shovel

spade

gardening forks

pickaxe

soil bag

flowerpots

brush cutter

wire mesh

scythe

garden gnome

rain boots

broom

axe

hose

lawn mower

hoes

insects

wheelbarrow

step ladder

hand saw

chainsaw

pruners

trowels

chopping block

WHAT GOES INSIDE
A HENHOUSE?

roost

straw and hay

poop

roosters

ladders

chicks

bowl feeder

grains

bucket

water bowls

hens

ants

eggs

chicken feed

mice

buckets of water

nest box

hay

perches

WHAT GOES INSIDE
AN ARTIST'S SUITCASE?

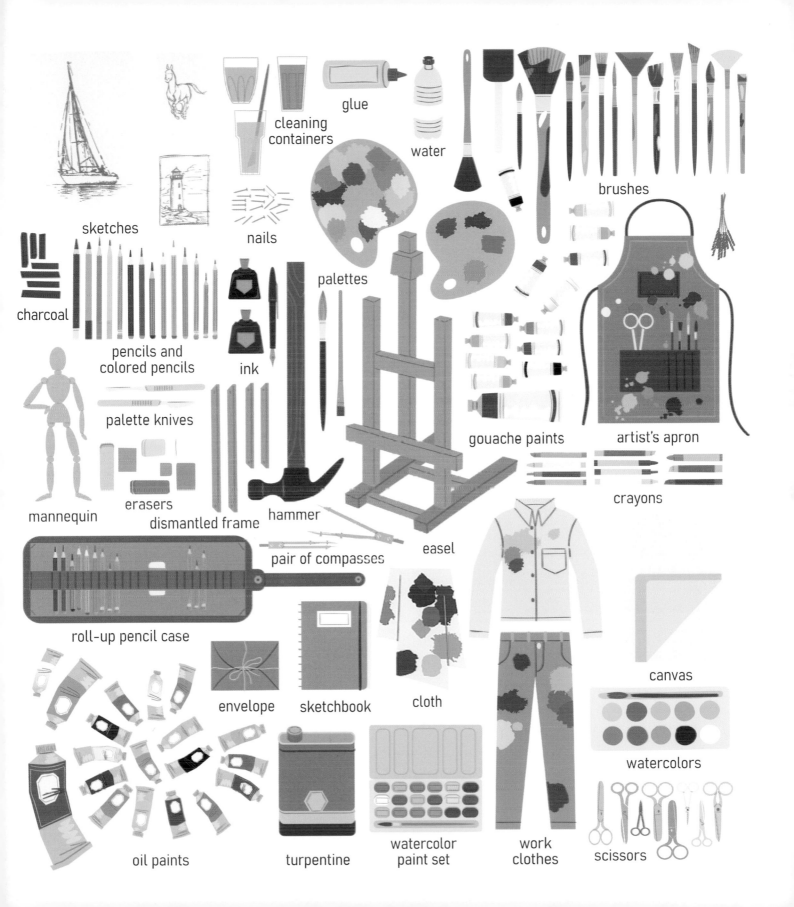

sketches

cleaning containers

glue

water

brushes

nails

palettes

charcoal

pencils and colored pencils

ink

artist's apron

gouache paints

mannequin

palette knives

erasers

dismantled frame

hammer

easel

crayons

roll-up pencil case

pair of compasses

canvas

envelope

sketchbook

cloth

watercolors

oil paints

turpentine

watercolor paint set

work clothes

scissors

WHAT GOES INSIDE
A FIRE TRUCK?

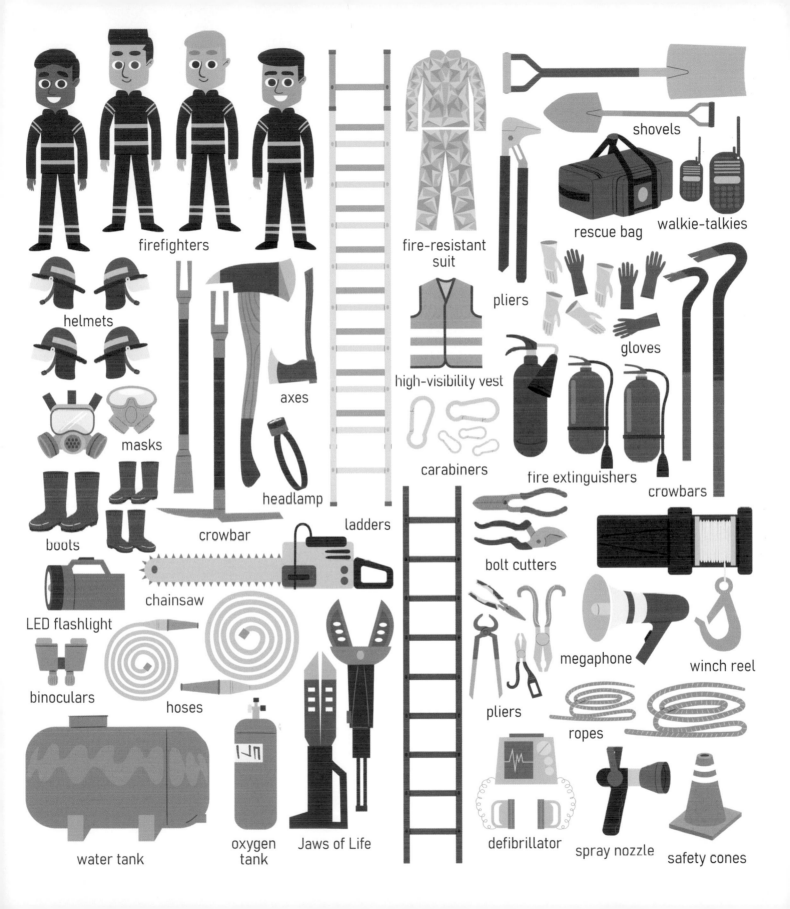

firefighters

fire-resistant suit

shovels

rescue bag

walkie-talkies

pliers

high-visibilily vest

gloves

helmets

masks

axes

crowbar

headlamp

ladders

carabiners

fire extinguishers

crowbars

boots

chainsaw

bolt cutters

winch reel

megaphone

LED flashlight

binoculars

hoses

water tank

oxygen tank

Jaws of Life

pliers

ropes

defibrillator

spray nozzle

safety cones

WHAT GOES INSIDE
A ROCK BAND'S VAN?

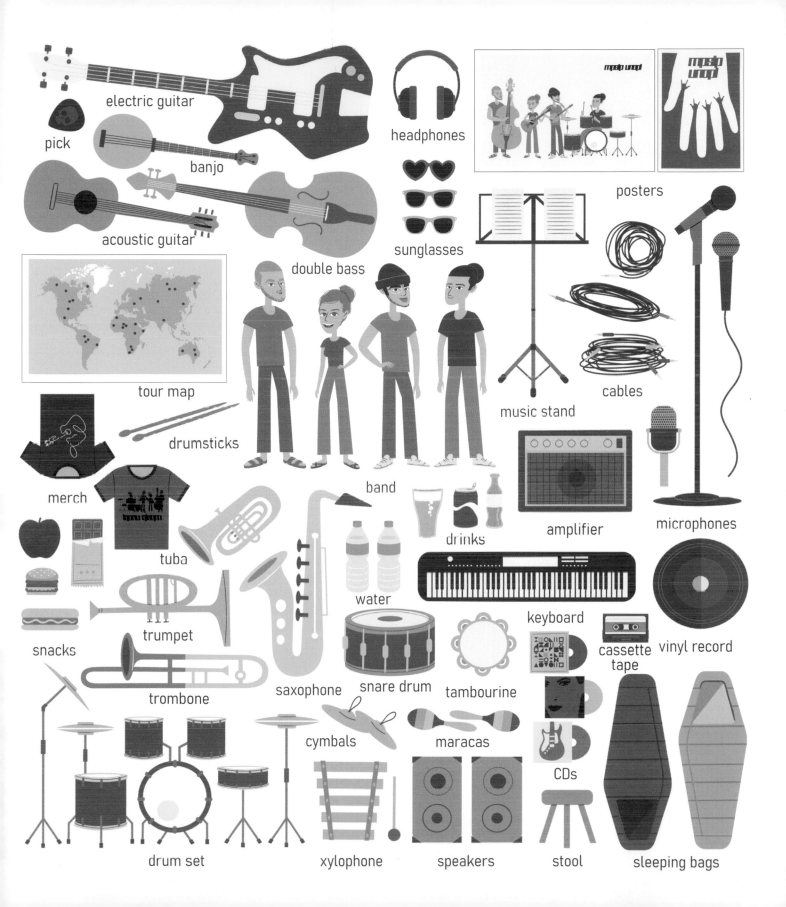

electric guitar

pick

banjo

acoustic guitar

headphones

posters

sunglasses

double bass

tour map

drumsticks

band

music stand

cables

microphones

merch

tuba

drinks

amplifier

snacks

trumpet

water

keyboard

cassette tape

vinyl record

trombone

saxophone

snare drum

tambourine

cymbals

maracas

CDs

drum set

xylophone

speakers

stool

sleeping bags

WHAT GOES INSIDE
A DOCTOR'S OFFICE?

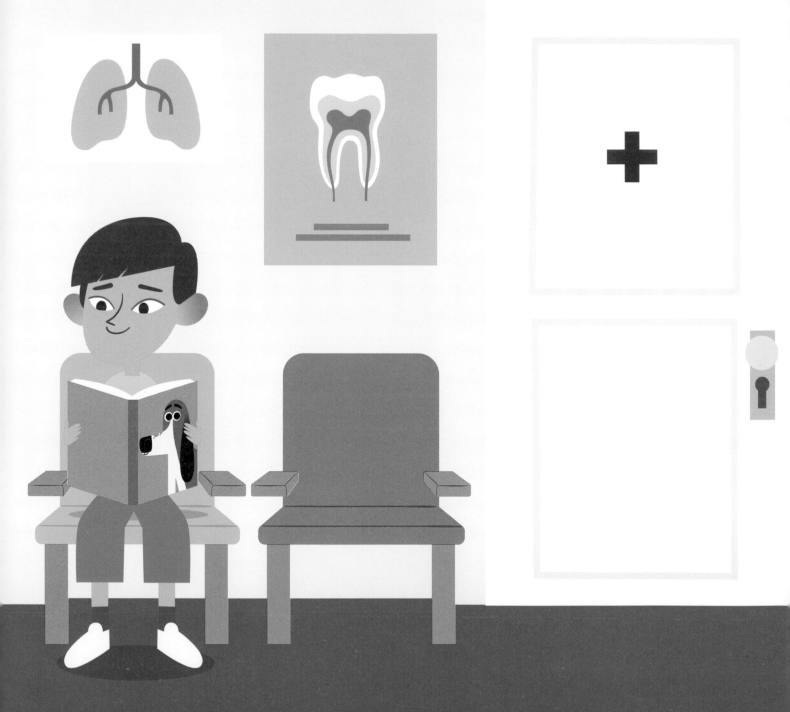

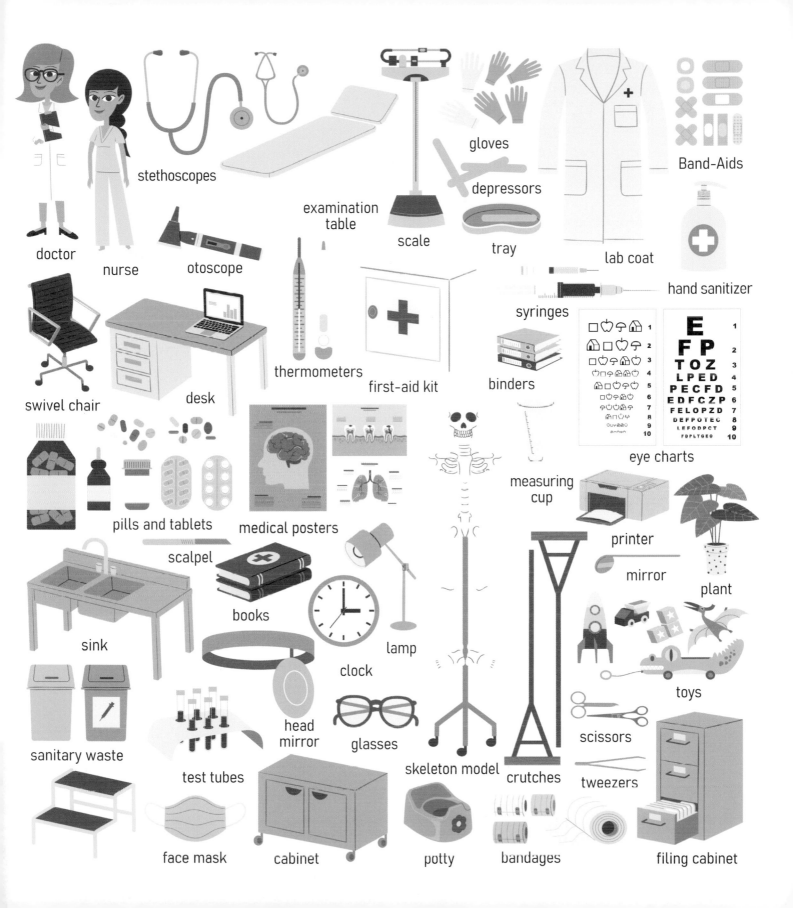

doctor

nurse

stethoscopes

otoscope

examination table

scale

gloves

depressors

tray

lab coat

Band-Aids

hand sanitizer

syringes

swivel chair

desk

thermometers

first-aid kit

binders

eye charts

pills and tablets

medical posters

measuring cup

printer

mirror

plant

scalpel

books

sink

clock

lamp

skeleton model

toys

head mirror

glasses

crutches

scissors

tweezers

sanitary waste

test tubes

face mask

cabinet

potty

bandages

filing cabinet

WHAT GOES INSIDE
A BOOK OF FAIRY TALES?

Hansel and Gretel

gingerbread house

Sleeping Beauty

princes

witch

seven dwarfs

swords

evil queen

wild rose

horse

jeweled crown

potions

mirror

Snow White

poisoned apple

wizard hat

crown

king

Peter Pan

queen

dragon

Cinderella

wizard

wolf

the three little pigs

glass slippers

Little Red Riding Hood

carriage

grandmother

Pinocchio

WHAT GOES INSIDE
A HIKING BACKPACK?

diary

stationery

guidebook

headlamp

socks

flashlight

tent

towel

sewing kit

sunglasses

hat

harmonica

jacket

matches

binoculars

sandals

teddy bear

compass

sweatshirt

sweater

T-shirts

trousers

shorts

raincoat

axe

first-aid kit

toiletries

sunscreen

repellent

water

mug

toilet paper

sleeping pad

rope

utensils

map

camera

sweets

water bottle

knife

pot

thermos

sleeping bag

gas stove

mug

mess tin

food supplies

canned food

What could have gone inside this gift?
What do you think?

© Designed by B4U Publishing for Albatros, an imprint of Albatros Media Group, 2022.
5. května 22, Prague 4, Czech Republic
Author: Magda Garguláková, Illustrator: © Federico Bonifacini
Printed in Ukraine by Unisoft.

ISBN: 978-80-00-06359-1